I0389747

Black Girl at the Intersection

Black Girl at the Intersection

by

LeTonia Jones

Accents Publishing • Lexington, Kentucky • 2023

Printed in the United States of America

Accents Publishing
Editor: Katerina Stoykova
Cover Image by Lakshmi Sriraman

Library of Congress Control Number: 2023931022
ISBN: 978-1-936628-98-8
First Edition

accents publishing

Accents Publishing is an independent press for brilliant voices. For a catalog of current and upcoming titles, please visit us on the Web at

www.accents-publishing.com

CONTENTS

Supplication 5.

Supplication 6.

Supplication 7.

Supplication 8.

For Love

Supplication

1.

When you see me throughout this day, ask me to circle with you. Ask me what it's like to be here, to be in this skin, and where I find joy. Ask me of my sadness and where the grief begins. Ask me if it ever hardens my blood.

When you see me, stay. Don't fear this intimacy. There is shared history in this glance. Please ask me how I see what I see and know what I know.

ORIGINAL SIN

She wears her secrets like skin
inherited from her father
the father before him
and the forefather
of them all

Vapid corporeal shells
housed grey veins
where blood should
flow

His translucent flesh held
desire for her foremother's
night skin—yearned for her
astral body to cover
his dissembled heart

He ravaged her body
took refuge in the power
of her dark light

He steeled himself in her
resolve for freedom
tried to escape his own
soul's captivity

He set rage onto her flesh
pounded his lies inside her
womb made secret
their bloodline

He placed price upon his kin
sold his own / sold himself
as if foreign
to himself

Original sin

He believed he could detach
from her night skin
and the seeds he bore
would never find a
way back to him

The origination of pain

Thin, weathered, and
cracked are the stories
that reach us now

I feel gale winds rush
through the veil
and my skin crawls
with secrets too

Lies rearrange themselves
as truths I silently
tell myself

I feel them penetrate me
whistle inside my ears
high pitched unbearable
and still I listen

Deception makes its way
becomes cells
membranes
pores

Skin borne of secrets
whispers and the sharp
teeth of my ancestry

gnaw at my face

My nose like hers
my lips like his
Africa and Europe

Most days the truth
of all of us
feels like a
lie.

GEORGE WALLACE ON REPEAT IN 2020

[redacted], [redacted] "Cradle of the Confederacy [redacted]

[redacted] Great Anglo-Saxon [redacted], [redacted] sound the drum for [redacted] generations [redacted] down through history[redacted]loving blood [redacted] and [redacted] chains [redacted]. [redacted] name [redacted] people [redacted] draw the line [redacted] toss the gauntlet [redacted] segregation now [redacted] segregation tomorrow [redacted] segregation forever

[redacted] sacrifice [redacted] children [redacted] be used [redacted] citizens [redacted] the nation's [redacted] safer [redacted] during [redacted] war [redacted] raid, [redacted] the people [redacted] for political reasons [redacted] build barricades [redacted]

[redacted] send this message back [redacted] we are [redacted] the heel of tyranny [redacted] fit the neck of an upright man [redacted] take the offensive [redacted] carry our fight [redacted] wield[redacted] power [redacted] WE, [redacted] determine [redacted] who shall sit in the White House of these United States [redacted] we give the word [redacted] race [redacted] honor [redacted] we will tolerate their [redacted] face no longer [redacted] let [redacted] judges put that in [redacted] power [redacted]."

A HATE SO STRONG

You refuse to wear
a mask yet

live to cover eyes
like mine

ignore the deluge
of tears in

blood soaked
black soil.

You ignore cries
for relief

while knee
in neck

take comfort
refuse to see.

You prefer us
covered in lies

ones you tell
yourself &

the lies we
have believed

myths you build
your monuments to.

You have always
preferred your hate

in the wide-open air
dangling from

Sycamore trees
torched inflamed

human flesh
left to rot.

You like it displayed
behind your badge

honored by the barrel
of your gun

protected by
your unions.

You love it recited
in your scripture

risen from your pulpit
rested in your religion.

You write the law
to benefit your own

codify it in gore
infuse it with rage

sanctified corruption
call it order

have the nerve to speak
the name of God?

Your hate suits you best
displayed in holes

through a spine
and in a colon

deep inside a chest
burrowed in a heart

holes in families
for generations.

You take solace in
blasts that deafen

those who want
to listen

and they who
came to pray.

Your hate loves
sunlight so

the children
can see

where it can
flourish

grow and live
into eternity.

You want to be immortal
yet have no idea of life

spew hate from your
uncovered mouth

contagious spread
the span of the world.

You refuse to wear a mask
and demand praise amid

destruction final pulses still
bodies caskets overflowed

the ground seeps red
while willows weep.

You take pride in your
right to infect

ravage maim
and ruin

enjoy the red in your
eyes seen as fury

flowing like molten lava
destroying futures.

You elect to white-
wash the past

believe you own
everything

live in the denial
you stole anything

created nothing
and it shows.

The veil is lifted so you
double down on hate

a hate so strong
it is hard to believe

this thing really
does end in love.

REASONS I PRAY

1.

how many ways can you ask
your country to stop
killing stalking surveilling
shooting & squeezing
life out of you

i stared at both of them
covered in caramel skin
they look like their
mother and their father

the oldest, 18, has a full ride
to college dreams
to become an engineer
has always been special
walked at 6 months old
talked 4 months later

the youngest, 16, does flips
walks on his hands
arrests you with optimism
loves animals declares time with
horses his best days
yet

they talk about their futures
hug on their mother
gently wrestle and love
on their father who
loves on them
right back

i capture this moment
as beauty in my
mind

2.

i knew them before they
took their first steps
now each of them steps
into manhood but
not just any manhood

they step into Black
manhood and my
temperature drops
under the warmth
of a Kentucky sun

the oldest awaits
a driver's license
my mind begins
to scramble

as we toss frisbee
reminisce and laugh
fear highjacks
my spine

Black manhood
is a rarity not many
Black boys make
it

i catch my breath
i pray.

A PRAYER FOR BLACK BOYS

Please let these Black boys
grow up and grow old.
Let them live. Allow them
to continue being their
parents' sons in spirit
and in flesh.

Let them be confused
have time to figure it out.
Let them grow wisdom
and go grey. Protect
them whether they
triumph or fall short.

Let these Black boys
walk alone on streets
and in parks in day
or at night. Let them
lie down under stars
with breath still
in their bodies.

Please let these
Black boys live.

Amen.

OVER AGAIN

i see him/her/me

                    i see us/we

Black bodies kissed by
night sky
beautiful
Blackness

smiling/disturbed
walking/dismantled
dancing/disrobed
joyful/disembodied

dead/displayed

                    as meaningless

at home on the couch
in parking lots and cars
on sidewalks and in
roadways

                    hands up/hands down
                    run/stand still

in morning and afternoon
beyond sunset
in slumber

                    no rest/a threat

all lives matter
unless they are
Black

all lives matter until
Black bodies say

us/we

too

PROMPT

Write the image you see
Use the word that comes next
Follow that word with another
word & another word

until there are no more words
until you can no longer
find another single word

i see a Black man's face
i see a Black man's face smashed
into the pavement—this time

his name is George
i see George's Black face smashed
into the pavement & his face

takes me back to my cousin's Black
face & what my cousin's Black
face must've looked like when
they forced him off
the cliff

i see white faced rage lashing
against *his* Black back
i see uniformed cop with
knee in *his* Black neck

i see my cousin's Black baby face
smiling back at my own Black baby
face

my eyes haven't fallen
upon his Black face
since we were
19

Write the image you see
Use the word that comes next
Follow that word with another
word & another word

until there are no more words
until you can no longer
find another single word

i see a grey casket
i see a grey casket filled
with a Black body—this time

it is Eric's Black body
i see Eric's Black body in
a grey casket—this is Eric
Richardson, not Eric Garner
Eric Richardson died
before Eric Garner

i see Eric Richardson's son
seated on the first pew
of the church

i hear Eric Garner's daughter
cry out from behind
a megaphone

i see me
i see me stand
i see me stand above Eric's casket
i see me sob and try to find words

i see me try to find words to lay to rest
another cousin, another Black body,
Eric Richardson, not Eric Garner

i do not know Eric Garner
Eric Richardson died before Eric Garner
i see Eric's mother tremble in grief
i see people fan her face to give her air

i see Eric's child
i see Eric's children's pain
i do know Eric Garner

i see Eric Garner's Black body
smashed against the pavement

i touch Eric Richardson's Black body
he is as cold as ice

i feel this cold as familiar
i have seen too much
touched too many—

too many Black
bodies

prompt

Write what it's like to try to
hang on to your
Black mind—

when there are
so many Black
futures

in the ground

A POET'S LAMENT

somewhere inside of me is a poem about a painted lady
who flits and floats along the contours of a Kentucky sky

or even a poem about the sound of laughter right before the
smell of burnt popcorn fills the air

there is a place inside me filled with poems about puppies that
court kittens & the beauty of my beloved's brown eyes

or one where i am a poet standing at the water's edge
holding a stone that won't sink this time

but i am not a poet there   i am not at water's edge

i am a poet who cannot escape the image of yellow crime tape
was turned away by flashing lights on a barricaded street

here i am a poet who can't shake the reality of a 10-year-old
Black boy named Landon once playing a video game

now in a casket after a bullet passed through his brain

BABY'S BREATH

clang, clang, clang
i hear the chains
before i see
the boy

i wonder whose
baby will waddle
into this
space

shuffle, shuffle, shuffle
i hear the feet
before i see
the weight

of the world
on shoulders not
yet broad enough
to carry a thing

scores of Black boys
are here called predators
called prisoners & property
never called children

i still smell mother's milk
on baby's breath
Black boys paraded
as men in jumpsuits

they wear orange and red
sorrow and pain
Black children denied
grief fear love
time

jangle, jangle, jangle
i hear the keys
before I see
a boy

locked away
locked inside
locked outside
of his right

to dream.

SUMMER SOLSTICE FOR EVERYONE?

What good is it to celebrate
the Sun without the warmth
of its rays

to want to reconnect with nature
without the color
green

to imagine a soul journey
without forgiveness from
the past

to chart a new beginning
without the voices of
anyone you love

what good are longer days
if spent shackled inside
the mind

what good are shorter nights
when all you have is
time?

Supplication

2.

Ask me what it's like to be on the brink of something and if I can feel it. Ask me what it's like to chew on this reality and if I can taste the astringence of lives half lived. Ask me how it feels to imagine survival through the eye of a needle.

Please ask me if it hurts sometimes.

A QUESTION OF BEAUTY

i am a little brown girl
i am cautioned too much
time in the sun
will make me a
Black
girl

no one knows
how i long
to be a
Black
girl

they don't know
i have always believed
sun-soaked skin
is a superpower

or how i love
to be in the
water

all
day
long

to emerge
with a body
that knows
it is filled with
Sunshine

they don't know about
the day i ate psychedelics
for the first time

& that i baptized
myself without
covering my hair

they don't know how
i felt there was a
rebellion
inside
me

nobody knows
that was the day
I became
beautiful

& still

no one knows
how hard it is
to never
forget
that
day

RUPTURED SINEW

photos on mantles
names
histories
legacies

we honor our
ancestors

children of people
purchased

nurturers on blood
soaked land

pride
work ethic
providers

photos on mantles
names
histories
legacies

to honor

not much said about
vacant eyes
absent smiles

witnesses of
atrocities

Black people
jerked into eternity

fallen to the ground
become ashes and teeth

they don't say what
that does to children
before they become

men and women
parents and grand-
parents
neither do they say
what happens to little
girls and little boys
left in their
care

until one day
they do say
and it
hurts

photos on mantles
names
histories
legacies

torn

BEGETS

an open wound walking
called husband
called father
called his

everything called his

pain pushed forward
stains
marks
haunts

for life

no emergency techs
no doctors called
blood spilled
innocence a myth

the wound
begets

BLURRED

she called her rapist today
called him Daddy again
called him daddy as if
that is all he had ever
been

she heard the lilt
in his stammer
knew he recognized
her on the line
felt his grin
permeate

space between

for a moment he *was*
Daddy again
simultaneous
warmth in two
hearts

for an instant the sound
of his belly laugh was
supreme punchlines
became a bond
she remembered
punch lines

the sound of her fist
muffled by his face
the bridge of
his nose
          collapsed
                    blood
                              spilled

her innocence
                    swam swirled
emptied into
                    a   toilet
drain
                    became

                    sewage

          he ran

she raged

shotgun barrel pointed
she stood her ground

she did not tremble

          he did

she called her daddy today
called him Rapist again
called him rapist as if
that is all he had ever
been

LESSON OF THE BITTER FRUIT

fed up haunted

that's how they
described her

at least

that's what
i recall

demons hovered above her bed

no laughter
in
between

smiles only
twisted her
face

fighting against life

that's what i remember
salty
aching
gritting
her teeth

gnashing until
the end
never healed

denial is a
thievish haint

& rejection
is the raven's
song

BLACK GIRL AT THE INTERSECTION

I see you skeleton walkin
flip flops flippin floppin
thong between bony toes

I see your blue jean shorts
wedged between the crack of
your barely covered ass

your ass bare hollow-cheeked
flesh droopin spillin into thin
thighs fallin into spindle-
shanked legs

I see you extend your raw-boned arm
scratch the back of your pebble like
neck run gaunt fingers through
parched hair

I see you Black girl skeleton
standin at the intersection see you
look left then right then left then
right

see you go nowhere

I feel the tensity creep up
our spines want to cry out
but realize my voice is gone too

I want to save you but
recall neither of us gets
out of this thing alive

We are Black girl skeletons in
need of attention—messes eaten
up by
a tension

We keep tellin mutha fuckas
we gonna break tellin mutha
fuckas to give us a break

but we are Black girls we don't
get breaks even when we are
broken no justice no peace

flip flop swivel left then
right then left then right
then nowhere

BEFORE I GO

s l o w m e down

m o m e n t m e now

b o d y m e through

(re)cover me

whole

memory / a story

presence / a salve

Please bless me

s a n e

Supplication

3.

I trusted what they told me. Felt the pain of the lie. I remember the stench of adoration decayed. Flesh of his flesh? I searched for a real father. I found more brokenness instead. I know the truth can hurt. Identity is ephemeral. And there is difficulty in the weight of blood.

Please ask me what it feels like to disappear in an instant.

DISAVOW

Once upon
a time
I wedded
loneliness
a coy specter
crept its way
inside / embodied
itself as my
beloved
hung heavy behind
my rib cage
moved upward
a phantom caught
fire in my throat
singed my vocal cords
nefariously betrothed
my language attacked
words twisted I spoke
in foreign tongues
reduced to wraith
my companion put
me to bed—whispered
I will always be
right here.
nemesis wrapped in cold
embrace / cradled in
shards of brokenness
my life deconstructed
my prayer   (re)member

SEVER

the sound of thread as it frays

the site of honey crystal

tongue on razor's edge

beat of contradiction

glass and shattered

beam

rain bow
on the

floor

A BODY NOT HIS OWN

After he turned 10
I think I heard
the word
seizure

When he was 19
I believe I
heard
them say

medically
induced
coma

He is 20
this time I
think

they said
the word

catatonia

Sometimes
the weight of
my phone
is too much
to hold
&

the ringing
in my ears
is too loud
to hear

Sweat in
my palms

feels like
an ocean
of anguish
&

a harsh glare
cuts me off
from
the sun
&

I notice my
fingers go
numb
&

I cannot
touch
him
&

I do not
know
if he
feels love

in
absence

I want to be
asleep as our
hearts shatter
into shards of
hope on
the floor

Today I think
I heard
them say
the word

profound

A faint voice
may have said
he cannot walk
he does not speak
he cries for hours

I may have
heard
her say
I chew
his food
for him

I think
he spoke
to me
last
night

I believe
he said

Auntie
I just
want a
chance

to become
a Black
man

RETROSPECTION

(in memory of losing Eric)

i remember you
and us

your little boy
cheeks

the way you averted
your eyes when

the crowd was
too big

i don't think anyone
would've described

you as bashful
but i would

i remember the
way you hid

behind your mother
when we first met

you were 2 inches
taller 1 year older

i remember when
they told us

your job was
to protect me

because i
was a girl

but it would be
me who

wished i could
protect you

i don't think anyone
would've described

you as defenseless
but i would

i want to know if
you remember when

we found out
grandaddy was a sinner

pages of nude white women
under his mattress

remember how we giggled
like kids because we were

kids who had just found
grandaddy's dirty lil secret

and do you remember the
drama of the snapping turtle

how you tried to
touch it

how it lunged and snapped
the tip of your finger

then we screamed
and you ran

and i ran right
behind you

do you remember
how they waited

until sundown to sever
the turtle's neck

and how we covered
our eyes

do you remember when
you were in the hospital

how you commanded if
anyone offered me crack

to treat them as if they
were trying to kill me

do you regret now how
you didn't get to turn 29

and that with one last
puff of smoke

you and me—
we vanished?

PUSH AND PULL

trees have done their thing again
turned shades of yellow, gold,
red, purple, and brown

leaves, once like soft green leather
now brittle, crumble under the paws
of puppies and walks in the park

temperatures drop, textiles change
scarves and hats, sweaters and jackets
corduroys and boots

beverages bear the weight of steam
in monogrammed mugs, whipped
cream dances atop freshly brewed
this and that

memories of a baby born in fall
espresso colored skin, lotion
scented coos, curly black hair
tiny life swaddled, safe

fall has come 16 times since
her face was more than an image
captured in a moment, frozen

now, woefully disappeared,
memories of homecoming
turned reality of homegoing

what should be, is not
what is, should never be

she should be 36, but
Sophia is dead.

memory pushes back, and time,
it brutally pulls forward,
without her
again.

A BLESSING FOR FAMILIES WHOSE LITTLE GIRLS NEVER COME HOME

When the wail begins
let it be full!

As your body concaves in disbelief
allow her name to form tightly
upon your lips.

May she hear you and
appear right by your side,
especially through this.

May you feel God's hand
cling to yours.

May your imagination
of her last gasps for air
cease in an instant.

When both besieged by
helplessness and rabid
with rage,

May you remember,
she was created by love
& so shall it be, she is
returned to love.

Finally, in the noiselessness
of the night, before you lay
her to rest,

May you forgive yourself again
and again and again.

Be you steeled in faith.
Be you girded by grace.
Be you reimagined as love.

And may you always know,
if it could have been
any other way,

it surely would have been
that way.

Supplication

4.

I remember the old sepia photo hanging over Mama Lettie's bed. It was of Mama Liza. I was short in stature. There was an eerie feeling of eyes in pursuit of me no matter where I moved. I stopped. I looked. I discovered my cheek bones and the shape of my eyes. I saw the broadness of my shoulders. One hundred years before me, the same distance from hairline to eyebrow. I found it was me (not me) framed above that bed.

I can still see Mama Lettie's tobacco pipes and her body age 98. The swing of my arms belongs to her. Her wit and depth of laughter, she passed to all of us. Her wisdom sounded like, "Don't start no mess, won't be no mess."

There was also Grandma Ada. Her sheepish grin and the light in her hazel eyes. We did not share blood. We shared love.

Please ask me about the memory of ancestors.

SWEET SMOKE

(In Memory of Lettie Vinegar Matthews)

I remember the sweet smell
of smoke wafting through
the air

The tobacco was stored
in a round tin on a
black shelf

There were two white
birds perched
above it

I thought they were doves
but she called them
weather birds

When it was humid
the birds turned yellow
then orange then red

As angry skies brewed
the birds turned pink
then blue then purple

I remember the portent
of dark clouds and the
scent of the earth before rain

She'd open her door
her voice firm & calm
as she herded us inside

She was the serenity
during a storm
she liked them quiet

Under candlelight she
urged stillness in
every one of us

The sound of water down
her gutters thunder
detonated everywhere

My childhood bones rattled
like windchimes—somedays
I forget I was ever a child

I was only as tall as the rocking
chair in her bedroom, the one in
which she watched her stories

She sent me to the black shelf
I caught myself in the mirror
I reached up and grabbed the tin

I still hear the *pop* of the lid when
the top came off, and I can feel
the sticky tobacco between my fingers

My eyes fell upon her pipes I
chose her favorite one—the black one
with a long stem and embossed bowl

I imagined the bowl as waves in
a black ocean filled with her
sweet sticky tobacco

I extended the pipe to her dark
brown hands covered in white ash
cracked skin on her knuckles

Both strength and care
lived in those hands
the hands that held her babies

The hands that caressed her
grandbabies the same hands
wiped tears from her great grand babies

Those hands planted flowers
threw corn to her chickens
picked apples

Beautifully worn & weathered
hands that swung axes and
prepared breakfast

There was black cast iron skillet too
heavy for me to lift but it never
stopped me from trying

I remember the sound of her
laughter and the sizzling of
white buttered bread

Tugging at her house dress
her deep voice would say
Girl, it's comin'.

I sat at her kitchen table
in the place set for me
white bread now golden

Toast covered in Bob White
syrup beside bacon sausage
fresh eggs from her chickens

She grinned as she fed me
watched me eat at her table
wanted me in her house

Attended to me playing in
her yard she enjoyed keeping
an eye on me

She took the pipe from
my hand and put
it between her lips

I chose her silver lighter
felt the ridges of the flint
wheel beneath my thumb

There was power as I flicked
the flame that lit her favorite
black pipe

I heard a crackle as fire touched
sweet sticky tobacco delight
ensued as she took short puffs

Rings of smoke became an air
show and she said, *Thank you.*
I remember this as sacred ritual

Mama Lettie is no longer here
I have three of her pipes but
not her favorite one

On each pipe I have placed
my own lips savoring the
spots she once put hers

I want to go back to her embrace
long for everything
I miss

Once upon a time I believed
she'd cook skillet toast covered
in Bob White syrup forever

Now I know there is
no such thing as
forever

A PRAYER FOR SWEETNESS

(In Memory of Ada Bell Jones)

She brought the cooker.
It was the big dark blue one,
speckled with tiny white dots,
the one with the wobbly wooden handles, the
one that reminds me of a starry night sky. This
cooker signified it was my time now.

She said, *this is the cooker Mrs. Ada used,*
the one she taught me to use. Now it is the
cooker I will teach you to use. This, the
cooker with over 100 years of love
and of lessons learned, and of life lived.

This cooker's been heated up, been filled
stirred in, and poured from
All this done with her hands
then with my hands
and soon with your own.

These apples—these are Jonathan's apples.
They are sweet and a little bit sour. Life can
be like that, you know—sweet and a lil sour.
I believe somewhere in between the two is
where grace lives.

Peel, peel, peel. Chop, chop, chop.
We don't mind if some of those chunks
are larger than others. That's what
makes it our apple butter.

It's how you know over 100 years of love
and of lessons learned, and of life lived
is going into this batch.

Now let's use one of those mason jars
over there on the counter. You're
gonna fill it up with some water. That
little bit of water, with all those apple
chunks is gonna go a very long way.

Let the apples boil down now.
We're gonna give them some time.
It's only with time you can really live
a life—make some mistakes, recover
And then turn around and laugh 'til your
stomach's tight and your cheeks hurt.

Come! Look at this! Apples boiled down
just right. Now we add the cinnamon
followed by the cloves. I love the smell
and the strength of cloves. Doesn't that
remind you of your grandmother, Ada?

Let's not forget the allspice. It's a
mixture of all kinds of goodness.
I'm not quite sure what's in it. But
then you know I like a bit
of mystery.

We are getting to my favorite
part. Did I tell you I like
doing this with you?

You are sweet just like all
this sugar. All my kids have a
sweetness about them.

Pounds of sugar, plus 2 cups. You've
gotta taste your way through this.

Sometimes it takes every granule of sugar
to get the sweetness of over 100 years
of love and of lessons learned and of
life lived.

Other times even a quarter cup
is just a bit too much. We risk it,
but we always wanna have
enough sweet.

My prayer for you is that your life
is more of the sweet. Not to shame
the sour, but as your mom, sweetness
is my prayer for you.

Perhaps this whole batch is a prayer?
Your grandmother was a praying
woman—faithful. And I am certain she
faithfully prayed for all of us.

Maybe it's her prayers that make this
apple butter ours? Maybe that's how
you know over 100 years of love and of
lessons learned, and of life lived goes
into this batch.

Be careful, those mason jars just came
out of that boiling water. Place them on
the towel. We must let them dry.

Now let's taste! How is it to you?
I think this is exactly what we want.

Let's fill all these jars now. It's ok
if some spills on the side. Just use

that cloth and wipe it down.
We want the rim to be dry.

Time to seal them up. We will seal
all those prayers and all that
sweetness into each one of those
jars. And once we hear the tops pop
our work is almost done.

I told you the best part is in
the sweetness. But I really think
it's in giving it away. This apple
butter is how we show we care.

We offer over 100 years of love
of lessons learned, and of life lived.

We share more than 100 years
of sweetness and we pass on
enough prayer to last a lifetime.

Daughter, I really love doing this
with you.

Supplication

5.

When you see me throughout this day ask me to dream; to close my eyes; to breathe in and breathe out. Ask me to create something with you and to share with you the deepest parts of me. Allow me to tell you about my heartbreak.

Please ask me if I ever had anything to trust.

THE SEER

who watches me
when I am alone?

who sees me
in the cloak of
my darkness?

can you tell me
what tears look
like falling out of
sleeping eyes?

are my nightmares
as dark as they
seem?

are they darker than
the others you
watch?

do you smell my sweat
before it seeps out
of my pores?

does it splash onto
my pillow or is that
my imagination?

do you know sometimes
i daydream of annihilation
speculate the many ways
it finds me?

do you know there is
a cryptic part of me

that welcomes melodies
of my own death song?

do you see the other
part of me that begs
that i stay here?

do you know my secret
is oftentimes i can't
discern which part of
me is worse?

do you watch my mind
wrestle with the truth
of me?

do you see memories of
the moment i was stolen
then secretly returned
as imposter of me?

were you there when
the glass shattered inside
of my prepubescent heart
and my vagina?

did you know the rapacious
intentions and voracious
appetites that were set to
devour me?

were you there when
i was written?

have you already
seen my end?

when the last page
is turned, will i get
to be free?

ELEVEN RISKS IN A DAY

1. to wake up

2. to leave my bed

3. to look in the mirror again

4. to entertain the voices in my head

5. to read a poem

6. to write a poem

7. to ask my mother for the truth again

8. to forget where i came from

9. to remember where i came from

10. to claim my own life

11. to fall asleep once more

OBSERVATIONS FROM A LITTLE BUDDHA IN MY LIVING ROOM

I sit
(you run)

I
wait for nothing
(you run)

I
embrace silence
(you run)

I
invite everything
(you run)

I watch

you run

SECRET SAUCE

drink bourbon black out
hide in plain sight
soften rough edges
try to tidy a life
the you that is a thought
will never be enough

a revelation only living
will allow you to
trust

Supplication

6.

When you see me throughout this day, please be with me steady. Allow me to lean into your warmth. Let me see your heart as I have offered you mine. Tell me you want to know more. Please ask me if there is more to share.

I will tell you, certainly there is.

WHAT SHE DOESN'T KNOW

She hasn't discovered
her wingspan

She doesn't trust her gills
to breathe her

Krakens trapped her
in their lairs too long

Her children screech
in echoes beneath the sea

She doesn't know she
can choose to hear them

She has yet to realize
she has already survived

BAPTISM

there is a wail inside me
a monsoon of tears
yet to cry

a mangled moan contorts
unfurls unleashes itself about
my gut

sometimes my back feels
like it has ached
for millennia

i once dreamed a microphone
at my mouth stilted words
riddled my tongue

an audience of me questions
unknown to myself
i cannot answer

behind me a body of water
i throw me into
the sea

wait for secrets to
engulf me instead
purified anew

my body crests atop
a surge fiercely
tossed to shore

fallen upon my knees
my head anointed
by sky

with my mouth wide
open i breathe for the
first time

on this day it is known
i do not have
to die

Supplication

7.

I have memories of playing in rain and mud. I have memories of sermons and hymns. I stood at the altar. And I read the Bible. I remember prayer and the tears. I remember wails and deacon's moan. Here, the church where I met Spirit. I also recall when church no longer fit. I ran inside a bottle. I know shame and agony and what it is like to fall. There was fire and suffocation. I needed rescue from the wreckage. There was smoke, embers, and so much debris. I had doubt. But I needed to stop. Sobbing on the floor, I cried out for help. Bright light through my window, I remembered Spirit never leaves.

Please ask me about grace.

WHY YOU FLY BLACKBIRD

(a response to Blackbird *by Nina Simone, 1963)*

You Be moonlight
sprinkled in stardust.

You Be the breath
of God.

Tis not you who
breathes that body.

Not you who hears
with those ears.

Not even you who
sees with sad eyes.

You Be the breath
of all that is living
everlasting.

Air through nostrils
filling up
emptying out
lungs.

Honey, that is
the breath
of God!

Will you take one
moment and leave
the chatter behind?

Take one moment
to marvel at all
you do not do?

Take no credit
for what is done
and not done?

Will you take one
moment to cherish
what breathes you?

Breaths breathed for you
Before you came up
from ash.

Before you grew your
own wings.

Do you know these breaths
have been loaned to you?

Count them among
the preciousness of
what cannot be owned.

The entire cosmos rests
in your sacred belly.

Starlight ignites your cells
electricity charges
through your veins.

The night sky chooses
your skin to press
upon.

Will you take one moment to
marvel at this wonder that
wonders not about you?

Instead, it expresses itself
as you, loves itself
in you.

Your greatest mistake
is to meet this breath
as though it was
in-formed by
man.

Your misstep is to
walk as if you know
where you are going.

Your gift lies in your
recognition of who
you really Be.

Sovereignty is grace
to amble & to play
to love & to name
to find & to believe

You are nothing
short of Divine.

So, you must fly
Blackbird.

You only fly.
can ever

COME BLACK WOMAN

darkness breaks again
this time foot atop
wooden floor
arms out stretch
come blink of
an eye

come thought
come doubt
come rumble
come tremble
come reverb

phase out

come frost
on blade of grass
come birdsong
come ease

blend in
parse out
sink down

crisp
lips dry
catch light

come bright
come yellow
come orange
come purple
come brown

come crunch
under foot

come heart
come beat
come blood
come pulse

come ground
come woman
climb upward

come pain &
squawk
come squeal
undone
sprawl out
take space

traverse
terrain
come Audre
come June
come Toni
come bell

come center
come full
come bellied
come birth

come love
come God
come power

come up
from

silence

FORGIVE ME MOTHER

forgive me mother
i became your judge

i misunderstood
confluence

i forgot a paradox of rivers
flow inside you too

believed only what i could
see & tried to lead you

when it was you who bore me
in pain

you forgot about you
for me

you named me
kept me

smiled at me
fed me

played with me
sheltered me

as best a young girl could

you honored my first words
wished for me a future

when few of your own
wishes had come true

forgive me mother
i jettisoned blame

demanded more from the
shoulders of a girl

too soon a woman
alone

forgive me mother for
i forgot to see you

i knew not how to be
until now &

you are still here
we are still here

to smile
to feed
to shelter
to play
to listen
to love

as best two
little girls can

I SURVIVE FOR MOMENTS LIKE THESE:

the surprise of a cool breeze
amid sweltering
heat

the sound of my mother's laugh
against the backdrop of her once
broken heart

the truth as it staggers from my lips
escaped from the bellows of
my mind

the witness of teardrops turned
rainbows in the beauty
of the sun

i survive for

the warmth of another
glance &

the infinite wisdom of
time

i survive because

i come from a people
who believed before
they could see

i survive because i am

as eternal as prayer
&
as ancient as the night.

Supplication

8.

When you see me throughout this day, ask me to dance, to spin, to twirl and to circle with you. Allow me to be human. Listen to stories about how I love and how I believe everything is only about love. Ask me if I want to know you. I'll tell you I do. I want to know into your marrow just as you now know into mine. Please ask me to be One with you.

I'll tell you we already are.

SISTER ONLOOKER

clippers, scissors, & razor blades
the smell of alcohol &
cologne

i am a fly on the wall &
these Black men feel like
home

today's topic is fatherhood &
how papas rolled away like
stones

i sit in my barber's chair &
witness Black boys actin'
grown

straight edges line stories &
define a strength that stands
alone

tales turned to sermons &
Black men rise to their
thrones

laughter, music & truth
as seeds of self-love are
sewn

i am a fly on the wall &
these Black men are my
home

SHELTERED AT HOME

apathetic to her own voice
fatigued by repetition
bored on bended knee

her lips worth more than
confession & regret

the *only* one in the room
the wrangle in her head
the ennui of isolation

she
wants
out

fruit of nuanced glance
electricity of impending risk

her
lips
hunger
for
the
soft
interior
of
anot*her*

SILENT INVITATION

one glance and i am
drawn to you
made alive

in an instant you
become the sweetest
thing i know

words unspoken
bodies say it all

we have been here
before on the edge
something made
unmade

in one gaze
i yearn to
take root

a lifetime of
memories out
of nowhere

i compost into
the depth of
your eyes

i hear the music
and beckon to
you

you
arrive

and

we
begin

WE DANCE ABOVE FLAMES

we dance in the midst of the fire
we go bright pink and yellow
we go green, orange and red

we dance above blue heat
blue flame this Black body
bends twists twirls
radiates dips out
of sight

we dance deeper
across thresholds
we move because
no survival without
rhythm / beat

beat that drum drum that beat
beat that body body that beat
beat that heart heart that beat
beat that mind mind that beat

mind that Soul revere this Soul

ancestral Soul
untouchable Soul

Soul stretches out and around
Soul be an ocean and a mountain
Soul goes peaks goes valleys
Soul goes home and
never leaves

no chains withstand
such mystifying heat
no say so
no say not so
this Soul transcends

this Soul goes
this Soul knows

we dance   above flames

A BLESSING FOR BLACK GIRL BECOME BLACK WOMAN

Black woman
royalty of Queens—they will
call you black & when they
try to feed you the poison
infused in each
letter of the word

May you always (re)member
you possess the power
to make the bitter
sweet

May you know you
have been chosen by the Sun
and you will shine through
whatever is defined as dark

Black woman
you are dreams made
manifest prayers answered
wails witnessed &
testimony
through
song

Be it known you were
spoken into life & life
you shall live

Your coiled hair
is your power

Your crown
is sacred

You shall not be
moved.

Blessed are you, Black Woman
and may you always cherish
the Black girl
who brought
you

here.

ACKNOWLEDGMENTS

Black Girl at the Intersection exists because of the love and support of many. First, I thank my beautiful mother for taking my very first poem written at 13 years old so very seriously. You set the stage for this moment. To my beloved brothers, we have survived a lot and without your courage and trust, I would have stopped long ago. To my grandmother, Dr. Lottie Lecian, thank you for being my example of a Black woman writer. Thank you to my best friend, Brent Leggs for always being willing to hear a poem fresh from my fingertips. To my best friend, Morrietta Nkomo your eyes on my first drafts meant the world to me. I thank you. Ashley C. Smith, thank you for your confidence in me and for your gentle nudges to "just get it done."

I offer immense gratitude to Tanya Torp and our brilliant writing BIWOC community and sisterhood, *Bloodroot Ink*. Writing what is with all of you has changed me from the inside out. Dr. Shauna Morgan and Dr. Dominique Hill, thank you for your loving critiques, care and your time. I hope each of you will be proud. Anu Kasarabada and Tosha Larson, I couldn't ask for a better and more beautiful hype team. Thank you for always showing up for me and believing these poems should find their way into the world. Dr. Chris Walling, your prayers for my highest good are always felt and received. Thank you for your love and support. Amy Lombardo, your enduring love and belief in me have long been my secret weapons against most of my doubts.

A very special thank you goes to Lynn Winter who believed this collection was possible before I did. To Leatha Kendrick, my first memoir and poetry teacher as an adult, you made me believe my words were meant for more than just my journals. To past and present faculty and staff at the Carnegie Center for Literacy and Learning in Lexington, Kentucky, I thank you for helping me to mature as a writer. The continuity of your generosity and encouragement helped grow a published poet. To the Kentucky Black Writers Collaborative, thank you for being the first to invite me to share from my manuscript. Without you, Jude McPherson, the title poem of this collection wouldn't exist.

Lakshmi Sriramin, thank you for your sisterhood and for the beautiful artwork you created for the cover. It tells the story of this collection even before a page is turned. You reside in my heart. Thank you to Devine

Carama for creating Poetry In Motion. My poetry changed and grew over time on your microphone.

To my publisher, poetry mentor, and friend Katerina Stoykova, I am blessed beyond measure for the wisdom you shared with me. The loving patience you have shown me throughout this process outweighed my fear. I thank you.

Finally, to Tywanna White, thank you for coming in during the final stretch and reminding me of who I am and why I write these poems.

ABOUT THE AUTHOR

LeTonia Jones is a lifelong Kentuckian who has used the alchemy of arts and activism for over 25 years. She has led public arts campaigns and projects with the purpose of centering the lived experiences of those pushed to the margins, while at the same time stirring emotions, facilitating space for insight, and moving audiences and communities toward greater acts of care and love.

In 2007, while employed at the Kentucky Domestic Violence Association, she collaborated with author and award-winning playwright Eve Ensler and V-Day to produce and pilot a two-week statewide arts and activism festival and awareness campaign to end violence against women and girls in Kentucky reaching 1.2 million Kentuckians. In 2009, she co-created and co-facilitated *SwallowTale Project,* which entered correctional institutions. The project culminated in a book called *SwallowTale Project,* which featured writings from incarcerated women in Kentucky. In 2020, LeTonia co-founded *Bloodroot Ink*, a writing circle for Black, Indigenous, and Womyn of Color.

LeTonia Jones lives in Lexington, Kentucky with her two dogs, Mojo and Peggy. *Black Girl at the Intersection* introduces her as a poet who believes acts of witnessing and acts of being witnessed are revolutionary.

www.ingramcontent.com/pod-product-compliance
Lightning Source LLC
Chambersburg PA
CBHW030157100526
44592CB00009B/324
9781936628988